I Can *with* Van

Other Books in This Series

S IS THE MOST DELICIOUS SOUND

R IS THE ROUGHEST SOUND

L IS FOR LEMONADE

CH IS THE MOST CHALLENGING SOUND

SH IS FOR SHINER

I Can *with* Van

Michelle McKee Marlow
and Cynthia Marlow

TCU Press
Fort Worth, Texas

Library of Congress Cataloging-in-Publication Data

Names: Marlow, Cynthia, author. | Marlow, Michelle McKee, author. | Skeels, Megan, illustrator.
Title: I can with Van / Cynthia Marlow, Michelle McKee Marlow ; illustrations by Megan Skeels.
Other titles: Hard-to-pronounce letters.
Description: Fort Worth : TCU Press, [2022] | Series: A series of hard-to-pronounce letters | Audience: Ages 3-8 | Audience: Grades K-1 | Summary: "Sometimes Michael gets stuck on a word. Come snuggle up with him as he discovers that music can lead him on the path to fluent speech. Following a musical note and a dream-visit with the the extraordinary pianist Van Cliburn, Michael goes on a wonderful journey to 'get the gold!'"-- Provided by publisher.
Identifiers: LCCN 2022004996 | ISBN 9780875658223 (hardcover)
Subjects: LCSH: Speech therapy for children--Exercises--Juvenile literature. | Speech disorders in children--Exercise therapy--Juvenile literature. | Articulation disorders in children--Juvenile literature.
Classification: LCC LB3454 .M3654 2022 | DDC 371.91/42--dc23/eng/20220225
LC record available at https://lccn.loc.gov/2022004996

Design by Rebecca A. Allen

TCU Press

TCU Box 298300
Fort Worth, Texas 76129
To order books: 1.800.826.8911

Book number six is extra special as it looks a bit different from the others in our series of hard-to-pronounce letters. In the first five books, we concentrated on articulation and hard-to-pronounce sounds. Book six is about something else: a condition called Dysfluency, also known as stuttering.

Did you know that roughly three million Americans, children and adults, exhibit dysfluent speech? Researchers have not confirmed why children and adults stutter; however, they agree that it is usually caused by something psychological, neurological, and/or hereditary. We would like to dedicate this book to all those who might be faced with a stuttering disorder. We wish for you patience and perseverance!

We would also like to dedicate this book to our Fort Worth friends at the Cliburn who helped make this book possible. There are many techniques used to treat dysfluencies today, but we find it most helpful to treat stuttering using a hum or musical note. This is the reason we have centered this book around Van Cliburn, internationally recognized as one of the greatest pianists in the world. What could be better than sitting at a piano, touching a key, and being reminded of simple techniques to help a child or adult maintain confidence while speaking?

Music is like painting in sounds. You take it into your inner heart and never lose it. It's eternally mysterious.

VAN CLIBURN

WORDS Can BE

Michael can say his S, L, R, Ch, and Sh sounds, but when Michael speaks, his words sound bumpy. Michael has a dysfluent speech disorder, more frequently known as a stutter. This causes Michael to get stuck on certain words or sounds when he is talking.

Michael grew up in Fort Worth, Texas, home of the Stockyards and the Van Cliburn International Piano Competition.

Michael's family loves playing the piano, and you can often find them in their living room, gathered around the grand Steinway piano, singing and playing songs. Every four years, Michael's parents welcome a participant of the Cliburn competition into their home, giving them a place to stay while they are in town to try to become the next gold medalist.

Tonight, the latest contestant to stay with them will arrive, and Michael is both excited and scared. From his bedroom, Michael hears his dad call up the stairs, “Michael, it is time for dinner. Wash your hands and come downstairs. Daniel has arrived and he cannot wait to meet you!”

Michael feels his heart start to race. He likes to hide out in his room when there are guests visiting. He is embarrassed to talk in front of people because of his stutter. But when it is a Cliburn pianist, his parents expect him to join, no matter what. "Hurry up, son," Michael's father hollers. "Dinner is getting cold!"

"C-c-c-coming!" Michael answers, hoping Daniel could not hear him.

Michael slowly walks down the stairs into the dining room.

Daniel stands to greet him with a handshake and a smile. "Hi Michael! How are you?" Daniel asks. Michael stares blankly. He feels the tightening in his throat. He has admired Daniel's piano skills on YouTube since he was seven and he does not want Daniel to notice his stutter.

Daniel presses on. “How old are you, Michael?” Daniel asks.

“T-t-t-twelve,” Michael sheepishly responds.

"Do you play the piano?" Daniel asks. Michael nods his head "yes" to avoid speaking. Daniel, sensing that Michael is a bit uncomfortable, asks if he would like to play a song together. Michael nods his head "yes" again. They head into the family room and sit down side by side on the piano bench.

Daniel asks Michael, "What song would you like to play?"

This question gets Michael talking and he quickly answers, “C-c-concerto n-n-number one by Tchaikovsky,” telling Daniel it was the first recording of his idol, Van Cliburn. Michael gets very excited when he talks about Mr. Cliburn, causing his stammers to interfere more than usual. He spouts off a number of random facts about Mr. Cliburn. All the while, Daniel listens intently, never once asking him to slow down or repeat what he just said. Daniel is very impressed with how much Michael knows about Mr. Cliburn.

They begin playing Concerto no. 1, and Michael feels calm immediately. He feels like he can trust Daniel. Daniel shows him kindness and patience, especially when his stammers give him trouble. When they are finished playing, Daniel asks, "Michael, would you like to be my special guest at the Van Cliburn competition tomorrow? I get to invite just one very important person to sit in the front row and watch my audition. I would be honored if you would come!"

Michael feels like he just scored the winning touchdown at the Super Bowl. He nods his head "yes" excitedly, agreeing to go to the competition the following day.

In bed later that night, Michael cannot sleep. "Why did I agree to go to the competition?" Michael asks himself out loud. Riddled with worry, he tosses and turns in his bed. He is afraid to go to the competition tomorrow because of all of the people that will be there. What if people find out that Daniel's special guest stutters? What if Daniel brings him onstage and he has to speak into a microphone in front of thousands of people? How will he avoid speaking to anyone the whole evening so that he does not have to reveal his big secret?

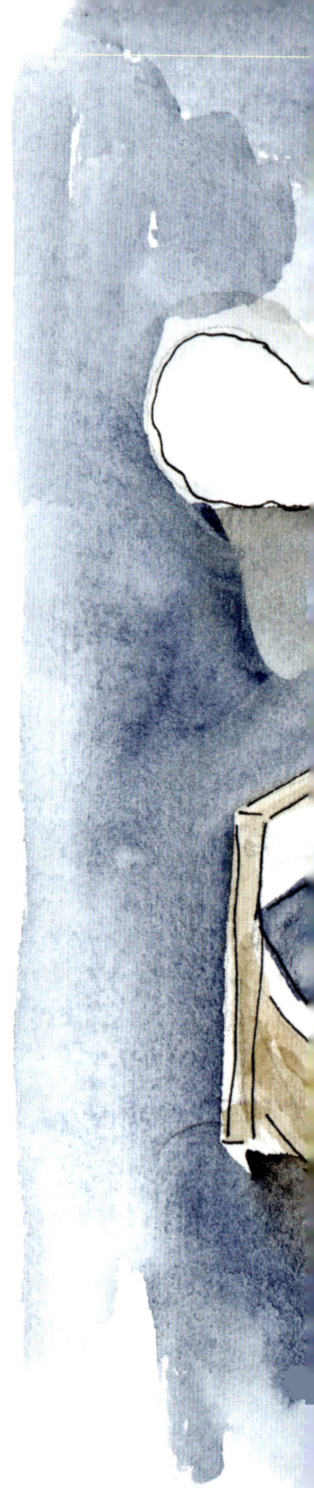

Finally, Michael drifts off to sleep. In the middle of the night, Michael wakes to see a vision in the doorway.

He sits up in his bed and rubs his eyes to try and get a better look. He cannot see the man's face. He can see that he has curly hair, and there are shadows of his long piano fingers on the wall. When the gentle-looking giant finally speaks, Michael knows it is Van Cliburn himself.

"I know you are scared," Mr. Cliburn says, "but you must face your fears and go to the competition. The music will help you. Hum with me." Mr. Cliburn begins to hum Louis Armstrong's "What a Wonderful World" and Michael joins in. Michael notices that when he hums, there are no stammers. His hums are smooth and there are no pauses or slow starts. Mr. Cliburn speaks again, "You see, when you hum, your vocal folds—also known as your 'speaking box'—stay open. This allows you to speak on top of your air like this . . . " Mr. Cliburn begins to sing "I see skies of blue . . ."

Michael joins in singing, "and clouds of white, the bright blessed day, the dark sacred night, and I think to myself, what a wonderful world!"

"Music is therapy, Michael. It's good for the soul. Your stammers will not go away overnight, but if you practice the humming trick I just showed you, over time they WILL improve. Be sure not to be hard on yourself. Be patient. Keep practicing. Speak with confidence. And the most important lesson of all is to never ever ever give up!"

And just like that,
Mr. Cliburn disappears.

The next morning Michael is up and dressed before everyone else. He is ready to conquer his fears and go to the competition. When they get to Bass Performance Hall in downtown Fort Worth, Daniel leads Michael to his front-row seat. Michael is nervous and excited at the same time. After three other auditions, Daniel takes the stage. He begins to play (Tchaikovsky) and Michael begins to hum. No bumps. No slow starts. Silky, smooth humming. Michael feels his confidence building.

As the song ends, the audience stands and cheers for Daniel. Daniel stands and bows, then walks off stage into the crowd to find Michael.

“How did I do?” Daniel asks, smiling from ear to ear.

“That was the best performance I have ever heard! You are amazing, Daniel! I am your biggest fan!” Michael says. For the first time in his twelve years, Michael completes a full sentence without a single stutter.

Michael closes his eyes and looks up to the sky and says out loud, “Thank you, Van. You gave me my voice.”

“I can with Van!”

Van Cliburn

JULY 12, 1934–FEBRUARY 27, 2013

Van Cliburn playing for his adoring fans in the Great Hall of the Moscow Conservatory during the Tchaikovsky Competition (April 1958). Photo courtesy of the Cliburn.

Born in Shreveport, Louisiana, in 1934, Van Cliburn became an American hero and an international icon heralded by US presidents, world leaders, and a vast, adoring public as one of the most persuasive ambassadors of American culture as well as one of the greatest pianists in the history of music. He was beloved not only for his gift as a brilliant musician, but also for his spirit as a great humanitarian.

At the height of the Cold War in 1958, Van Cliburn—a twenty-three-year-old Texan—won the first International Tchaikovsky Competition in Moscow, a contest designed to demonstrate Soviet cultural superiority. When the judges asked permission of Soviet leader Nikita Khrushchev to give first prize to an American, Krushchev asked, "Is he the best? Then give him the prize!" Cliburn returned home to a tickertape parade in New York City, the only time the honor has been bestowed on a musician.

Instant fame begat a career that included the first Grammy® for classical music; the first classical album to go triple platinum; record-breaking concert ticket sales; and performances for every president of the United States from Harry Truman to Barack Obama as well as for royalty and heads of state from around the world. In 1962, a dedicated group of Fort Worth volunteers held the first Van Cliburn International Piano Competition in his honor; the competition is now widely recognized as one of the most prestigious in the world.

Michelle McKee Marlow's passion for her private practice in Fort Worth has led her to work with hundreds of children from infancy to high school who have speech impairments. Her passion inspired her sister-in-law, ***Cynthia Marlow***, to earn a master's degree in communication sciences and disorders. Internationally, Cynthia has been the head of special education programs, a dyslexia specialist, and a speech pathologist, and has led professional development seminars for several international schools in Europe and Asia.